I AM PROUD

By JBus
Illustrated by Kara Matters

Library For All Ltd.

Library For All is an Australian not for profit organisation with a mission to make knowledge accessible to all via an innovative digital library solution. Visit us at libraryforall.org

I Am Proud

First published 2023

Published by Library For All Ltd
Email: info@libraryforall.org
URL: libraryforall.org

Our Yarning logo design by Jason Lee, Bidjipidji Art

Original illustrations by Kara Matters

I Am Proud
JBus
ISBN: 978-1-923063-00-6
SKU03376

I AM PROUD

We respect and honour Aboriginal
and Torres Strait Islander Elders past,
present and future. We acknowledge
the stories, traditions and living cultures
of Aboriginal and Torres Strait Islander
peoples on this land and commit to
building a brighter future together.

I am proud to be an Aboriginal person.

I am proud of my heritage and connection to the oldest living culture on earth.

I am proud to have a culture that has survived over such a long time.

I am lucky my family keeps our culture alive by teaching me.

6

My grandad teaches me how
to carve spears and axes to
hunt with.

My grandad and dad say that
I can't go hunting with them
until I am older.

I watch them.

I see them come back with tucker for our dinner to celebrate with our family.

One day, I will be helping them and that makes me proud.

My mum teaches me traditional art. She says it will teach me patience.

I like feeling the paint in-between my fingers.

We paint on wood, crab shells and paper, too.

We create beautiful, colourful art.

My mum says traditionally art was used to tell stories and pass information to the next generation.

My dad and uncles teach
me how to fish and carve
out parts of the rocks to
catch fish in the tide.

We use nets to
catch crabs and
my dad spears
fish in the water.

I must be quiet,
they say, so we
don't scare the
fish.

We aren't allowed to take more than what we need to eat that night.

They say that mother nature needs to have some for herself so the land can thrive.

My aunties teach me how to be respectful. They growl at me when I am being cheeky or disrespectful. They teach me how to behave, and how to give and share.

I know when I need a hug and advice, my aunties and uncles are always there to guide me.

My Elders teach me how to keep culture alive.

They share with me traditional dances for ceremonies and stories.

I love hearing the stories of our ancestors' ways.

They always teach me something important to help me as I grow older.

My mum and aunties teach me about nature and the environment, and how we can connect with the land.

They teach me how plants can help me when I am sick and injured.

I sit on the land.

I listen deeply.

I hear the birds, the insects buzzing around me, the sway of the breeze in the trees.

I smell the fresh plants around me and the salt air of the water nearby.

I feel the vibrations of the earth in my heart and hands as I breathe in and out.

I am connected and I belong.

I am home.
I see my Country.
I see my people.
I see our strength.
I see my culture.
I see me.

I am proud.

You can use these questions to talk about this book with your family, friends and teachers.

What did you learn from this book?

Describe this book in one word. Funny? Scary? Colourful? Interesting?

How did this book make you feel when you finished reading it?

What was your favourite part of this book?

download our reader app
getlibraryforall.org

About the contributors

JBus is a Kabi Kabi woman from Queensland and lives in Brisbane. She enjoys being at the beach with her family, creating art and singing.

Kara is a Noongar artist from Albany, Western Australia, with extensive experience in acrylic painting, digital art, illustration and design. Inspiration comes to Kara in all forms; she draws from the Earth, the Ocean, and what connects her emotionally to Country and soul.

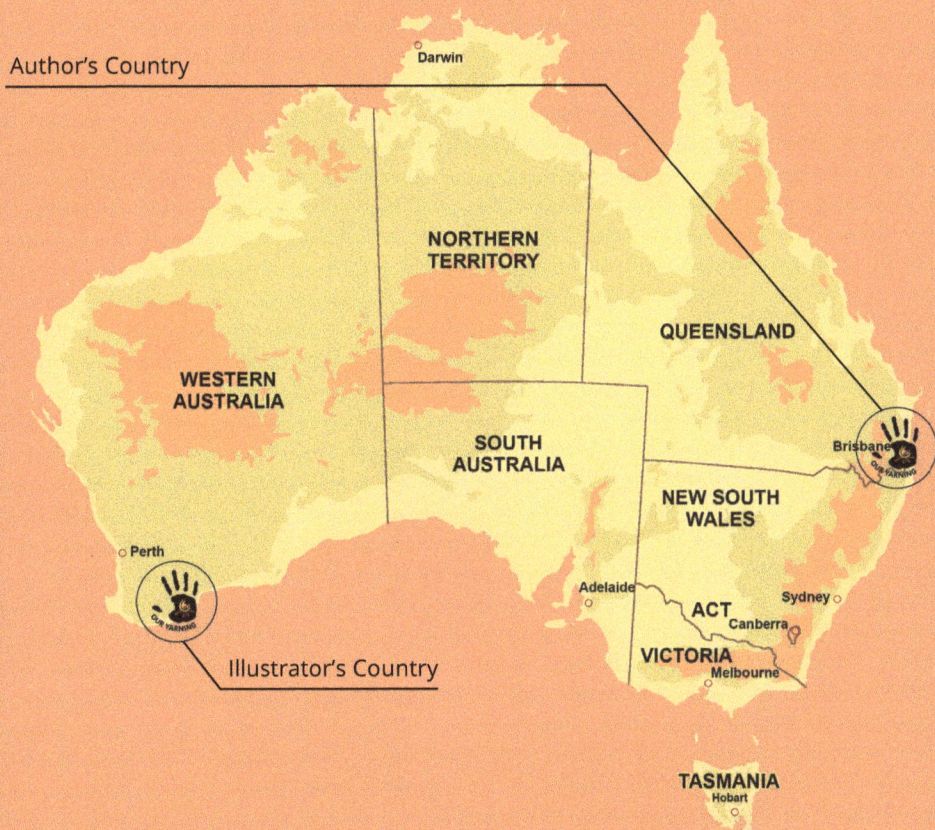

Author's Country

Darwin

NORTHERN
TERRITORY

QUEENSLAND

WESTERN
AUSTRALIA

SOUTH
AUSTRALIA

Brisbane

NEW SOUTH
WALES

Perth

Adelaide

Sydney

ACT
Canberra

Illustrator's Country

VICTORIA
Melbourne

TASMANIA
Hobart

Our Yarning

Want to discover more books from this collection? Our Yarning is a collection of books written by Aboriginal and Torres Strait Islander peoples across Australia.

We know that children learn better, and enjoy reading more, when they see themselves in the stories, characters and illustrations of the books they read.

To download the app, visit the Google Play Store on any Android device and search 'Our Yarning'.

librarleforall.org

www.ingramcontent.com/pod-product-compliance
Lightning Source LLC
Chambersburg PA
CBHW042340040426
42448CB00019B/3355